The Story We Are Becoming

Sakina Sakerwalla

BookLeaf
Publishing

India | USA | UK

Dedication

To every reader finding their path, one page at a time.

Preface

This collection of poems is a journey—one that spans the landscapes of identity, patience, and the quiet moments that shape who we are. It is an exploration of what it means to exist, to struggle, and to grow. In these pages, you will find reflections on the fragility of time, reflections of perseverance, and the quiet strength in accepting who we are becoming. I invite you to reflect alongside me on the complexity of our shared humanity. They are a reminder that the journey of self is never linear, but a collection of fragments that, when pieced together, form a whole that is uniquely our own.

Acknowledgements

This book would not have been possible without the unwavering support and encouragement of my family—your love, support, and encouragement are my foundation.

Before Dawn

An eerie chill engulfs me
before the arising dawn wakes
almost as if I can hear the rise and fall
each breath of the sleeping people

Closing my eyes, indulging in the echo
a reverberating silence that washes across the land
tingles skittering across my skin,
is this peace?

Do I feel safety knowing I hold the power
for the unlimited possibilities in the day to come
before the people wake and the cycle repeats
the same people who woke yesterday and nothing
changed.

Except me.

Push and Pull

Maybe you don't notice the slight lag of steps
The half-second hesitation before standing up
Or maybe you do. But an indifferent ignorance
to the stiff legs that take some time to move
the dull ache or inflamed veins.
What do you see in reality?

Do you see the battle waged beneath the skin?
A helpless guilt and an ambitious will
Dragged down by leaden limbs
The silent protests of a weary frame
Push and pull. Each a small victory within
You shall never know.

The urge to move forward but the hold
keeping you in place. I can see the goal
I want to get to the end. But somehow
I can't seem to take a breathe and *move.*
It's not fear. It's not doubt. It just *is.*
Weight without shape, pulling from within.

You shall not know nor experience, I pray.
This unexplained phenomenon of pain
But I ask that you take a moment –

Look. Look beyond the surface, if you dare
You won't see the helpless girl standing there
but a survivor's gaze will meet your stare.

Choices

That moment.
The one second.
The one fleeting thought.
It comes and goes so fast, was it even there?
The border between rage and calm. A line
at the end of the horizon.
Distinguishing the sky from the land. The sunset from
the ocean.
A wall.
There's an urge to choose the raw untapped power.
The one that knows no boundaries.
My muscles twitch with restraint.
Unrelenting and focused energy. Charged.
Ready to strike like a bolt of lightning.
In that same moment, the dull throb, too stubborn to
budge.
I can't move my feet or utter a word. Jaw locked.
It holds the barrier in place. A deep abyss of cool
sanctity.
The voice that tells you to let it go. Use your logic.
But you can't pay too much heed.
Which allure?
Strength to choose, and even more strength to not.

Is this a test?

Is this patience? A choice of my will?

Which will you choose?

Towns of Nowhere

Armies of sleek rainbow fishes
roaming the obsidian waters carefree
Flecks of flesh, flashes of light, with speed they glide
Amidst the abyss of blues and black with no place
outside
The water entraps them. Forces them down.
With failed attempts to rise above the surface they
struggle and squirm
To break free from the hands above.
That's what I picture when I see you.
In the middle of this barren land, a drying river with
Dying yellow grass on the banks
and empty lonely trees. No colors to keep you happy
No mountains to keep you grounded
No chirps of birds, those who have fled
Escaping the snare that keeps you here
It's a fleeting thought as my car passes through
Jostling on the pebbled road
Like a wave that rises and falls. My sighs are for you.
Where are you in the world?
Is this the end, to reside in this dreary town on the side
of the road
But then again, where are the rest of us?
Are we all just scaled fishes swimming in this

Deep abyss we call Earth

Those who look upon us from above, scattered atoms orbiting

A center we cannot find.

I look back at you as you become a speck in the horizon.

I fade away. Following the direction carved by man.

Still, looking for the way out.

Somewhere? Nowhere?

Keep Going

Climbing

The pyramid

Of life, trying

To reach the top.

But what is the top?

Is there an end? I don't

see it, but I keep going and

when I look down and see endless levels

that I struggled to climb. Massive bricks. Unmovable
obstacles.

Then turn my head up again, and continue towards the
unknown.

The unsettling feeling in my stomach growing. A queasy
ache that rolls

from side to side. Sweat drips down my jawline in
anxiety. Back muscles

aching from trying to stay upright. Feet blistering from
the rocks that poke into my skin. Head

bursting from the rollercoaster of sorrows and joys. I
continue. Repeatedly chanting prayers that

keep me grounded. Telling myself that it's not the top I
want to reach, when that's all I want.

The Sounds of Nature

I hear you little birdie
Chirping away in the giant tree
Looking to find you
In vain I can't see
Hidden within the hues of green dusty leaves.
Your tune is habitual
Every day I wake up to the constant high pitch chirps
Deciphering what you may be saying
or making it up as I go
You're singing about the green and gray
or the world you see, through the haze
The dust and dreary clouds of smoke
The pungent smell of petrol
I strain to understand, maybe I'll catch
A word or two
But the truth is simple
You're just a bird, singing your song,
That's where your voice belongs.

Pure

It floats aimlessly,
a white airy cloud, lined with silver. There are
no burdens.

Refreshing, just as gulping
a cold glass of milk,
after warm gooey cookies.

Stainless, cotton, white
it sparkles in the scorching sun
ready to be painted.

All encompassing,
a crystal, clear all the way through.
A rainbow, bringing color to every dull sky.

A hush between pulses,
a form without an anchor,
it sounds like the echo of something not yet named.

You Bloom in Day Light

A soft petal unfurling in the morning dew
Basking in the morning sun, you claim your place—
Not rushed, not forced, just fiercely grown,
A strong back. Not stubborn, sheer will.
You rise when you see the Day and bloom.
With every ray, it calls to you
What are you? What am I, it makes you question.
You are the seed that flew through the storm
Planted roots in a land unknown.
When it was time to break the walls and rise above
you grew, and grew, and grew.
In the womb you nurtured
and finally we saw the spring bloom.
Your petals pulse with living hue—
Electric reds, defiant blues,
A burst of orange, bold and bright,
A riot kissed by morning light.
Each shade a voice, a skill, a flame—
A brilliance begging to be named.
You rise, unshaken, shaped by will.
A garden waits, a path ignites—
Step forward now. Unfold. Take flight.

The Fire We Forget

I am the kind of fire that waits in stone —
slow-breathing, woven in ember hush,
warm enough to stay, but never to chase.

There is no frost in me, only what settles
when presence is mistaken for permanence,
when the air forgets who held it through winter.

I do not bloom to be noticed;
I slip through unseen seams in the earth,
choosing shadow where it listens more than light.

My flare is not for applause.
I move where I'm needed,
even if no one sees.

Let the watchers wait for signs they understand.
I am fluent in the language of what remains,
of what lingers after the echoes are gone.

And if that is too quiet for the world to bear,
then let the world watch and learn
how silence can forever burn.

Glue

A wrinkled paper will never be wrinkle free
You can fallen and erase but it will not be.
A mirror cracked, splaying hundreds of lines
Shards that draw blood
The reflection cracked
an image distorted
Is this the truth in fact?
Are we not perfect reflections but
shredded souls?
How do we fit the pieces back together
What is the perfect image
who will glue the remains
       and make sure they stay intact?

In the Void I See

In the fleeting moment when words are unleashed
the void is filled with unseen waves
to some it's gibberish, a blur of sounds and clicks
but I understand.
I understand the words spoken. The ones yelled and ones
cried.
The ones you see and the ones unheard.
I can hear the whispers of your soul.
It speaks to me in an unspoken language,
One that echoes in the silence between breaths
In the pauses that hang in the air like a question
unanswered
Speak to me and let your heart be free
share you secret stories and happy memories with glee.

Broken Roots

(Inspired by "Twenty-Four" by Jane Wong)

It's time to break my roots from yours.
An unhealthy habit to grow together
You became a weed in a garden not meant for you
I regret giving my heart to you
Regret that I did not see
How unfaithful your friendship can be
Drowned in the deep blue sea
Were any of the words true?
Promises of friendship and loyalty
Stories and secrets shared in the dark,
Whispers that once felt like they held spark.
You stayed silent when I needed truth,
Letting the words fall, uncaught, uncouth.
In your silence, I found my answer,
A truth that burned, a quiet cancer.
Now I see, I don't need your lies.
and meaningless conversations
Spineless and askew
Friends forever? I think not.
Lost is that bond you sought
Stay forever drowned in thought.

While I break my roots from you and go
From here on out I will grow, grow, grow.

Deadlines

Are we ever ready before the deadline?
Tick tock. Tick tock. A timer set, ingrained.
It runs in the back of my head, unseen, unknown.
Yet, as it draws near, there's a shift in gear.
Run run run!
Get it done!
Pressure increases and the pace picks up
with the deadline looming, no time to stop.
Every second, a race against the unstoppable clock
we chase the minutes, caught in between.
But when it's done, and the timer fades,
we breathe, we laugh, and the tension fades.

Layer of Patience

Sometimes it feels like it will slip through the
thick shield that I built up, brick after brick.
I force it back, the pressure of anger,
my eyes blink fast, just to make sure that you
don't glimpse the water building up behind
the soft eyes that cry when you're not around.
I won't lie when you ask if I'm alright
Even though you know the answer. Patience
wears thin and the wall instantly crashes
like waves rolling against the rocks building
their momentum to finally splash, thrash
against the cliff and rise above the edge.
Water droplets spray all over and then
drop down with a thud settling into
the cracks of the brick wall. Waiting again.

In the Clouds

Above the land and snowy mountain caps,
I see the shining sea, deep and angry,
A churning mass of power, raw and untamed,
It's a sight to behold—
The wrath of nature and the quiet of the sky,
Two forces in perfect contrast yet in sync.
Floating in a cloud,
In a plane I glide,
Watching in awe as the world slips away.
The sky wraps me in its silent embrace and
float.
Below, a kaleidoscope of hues—
The deep reds, the golden glows, the sun drifts.
An original piece of art.
What are we but flecks in the universe?
A brief flicker of light in an endless abyss
And in the midst of it all,
We find meaning,
In the stillness of the clouds,
In the beauty of a fleeting sunset.

Burn

It starts out with small itch in my ear.
Like an ant has crawled inside, and keeps moving in
circles.
A slight buzzing noise,
an eerie moment where
nothing moves and I stand still, empty.

My thoughts ignite.

They pulse back and forth, slamming into the sides of my
head
Veins throb, trying to hold together their walls.
There's an erratic heartbeat. Disturbing every sensory
nerve.
Tingling in my fingers and needles in my toes.
Blood whooshes towards every limb.

Rage.

It's like a firework
Whose only color is red
A whirlpool of thoughts swirling in my mind,
of things I should have said or done

But I hold it back.

I watch the firework fade away into
the black abyss of nothing it came from

until it vanishes.

And there is -

only the ant.

Know Thyself

I'll ask you what you think about me
and I care what you say
if you think I'm purple and royal
or boring and gray

if you see a flicker worth saving
or a candle guttering out in the breeze
if you hear a melody rising
or just noise lost among the leaves

I'll hand you a map of my heart
with roads I haven't traveled yet
and wonder if you'll trace the rivers
or only circle the regrets

I'll ask you what you think about me
because sometimes I forget to know
whether I am a garden growing wild
or a field buried under snow.

Jitters

An erratic pulse, a throbbing vein
nervous energy pulses through my trembling hands
and sweat glistens against my heated skin
But a smile tugs at my lips, unsure what to be
nervous or happy? Maybe both? There's a sense of
challenge. A thrill I seek.
The world spins with possibilities, bright and close.
I feel the flutter in my chest rise,
A weak laugh escapes before I can stop it.
The air feels thick, but I'm breathing in.
My legs tremble like wobbling jelly, but I stand tall.
I trust the process, let go of doubt.
Good things are coming, they always do.

One Milestone at a Time

Reach.
Stretch out
Push yourself ahead
The journey is unknown
yet the path is adventurous
step by step each victory counts.
Even the tiniest change, the smallest range
be grateful to be able to moving on
celebrate each milestone. Bask in the moment and let
it all in, every little victory, every moment of growth.
take a breath and feel thankful for what you have
achieved
Thankful. In each breathe and each beat of my heart. To
continue ahead.
With every step forward, find appreciation for the
journey
For this path, for today, for every small milestone made.

New Beginnings

How do we look for closure?
To bid goodbye to something
That we love too much but want it to end so
something new can begin.
To keep that last bittersweet taste alive
As long as we can,
Until it becomes a faded memory
And you start to question if it's still there,
Or it's your imagination.
Maybe it's the taste of nostalgia,
slipping through our finger like sand.
We try to hold it close, not wanting to forget,
but afraid that keeping it will hold you back.
Do we mourn the end, or rejoice in the possibility?
In the midst of goodbyes,
Hoping they'll guide us toward something brighter?
Perhaps the closure we seek
Isn't in the ending at all,
But in the moment after, where we get to decide
our new beginning.

To Live and Write

After so many deaths I live and write
With the ebb and flow of fight and flight
Now in this age I have again grown
To wander and look back at what the world has shown

Beyond the savannas bluer than your dreams
the magnolias, honeysuckles, and horizon seams,
A young girl wanders lonely like a cloud
lying, thinking, covered in snowy shrouds.

She thinks of winter and the Christmas lights
Giddily awaiting the season of colors so bright.
Young and naïve, filled with hope
The little one grew into a fine lady, strong as a rope
With knots her in her life she was still not tangled.
A poet she became, and words she handled

She is happy she is loved and beloved
In a place she does not remove nor be removed
Filled with wisdom and experiences of love
Heartbreak and reality, the treasured trove.
Compare with her, women, if you can.
She prizes her love more than whole mines of gold.

Men lacking dignity are seized by pride
Maybe a friend is the one to confide?
Love is most astonishing
because the proper place, the right moment, it's all about
timing
It cannot be taken quietly, unheard or unseen
These crimes have accounted been.

Perspective changed her way to see
the yellow-leaved waterlily,
the green-sheathed daffodilly,
and how they tremble in the water chilly.

When it's time to wither away
Like the leftover snow in May
She closes her eyes to start again
Break the ties of the past to gain
And again writes.
Writes, writes, writes.